ELSEWHERE

ØYVIND HJELMEN

KEHRER

FOREWORD
BY TRACY XAVIA KARNER

With transcendent vision, Øyvind Hjelmen has created
a seductively beautiful world in ***Elsewhere****.*

THE PHOTOGRAPHS OF ØYVIND HJELMEN

An ongoing, life affirming series, *Elsewhere* is Hjelmen's soothing response to the anxieties and distress of contemporary life. Lone figures pause in nebulous moments between what was and what will be. Shrouded in fog and bounded only by painted lines, laden trucks head down unknown roads. A full moon guides wandering pilgrims onward. Abandoned stairs and empty chairs mark the shared journey. Above all, *Elsewhere* is a visual travelogue of a life well lived — full of exotic, yet seemingly familiar places, voyages of adventure and memory — a diary of the shadow and light that makes up a year, a day, a moment.

Øyvind Hjelmen creates a passage across continents and through time, only to reunite us at our most humane desire for beauty and wonder. An exacting craftsman with a poet's soul, Hjelmen's gelatin silver prints call to mind the pictorialist tradition yet with contemporary sensibilities. Whether in individual prints or nestled in fine, handcrafted leather folios, moments of wonder and delight beckon — sometimes crystal clear and other times hazy, but always deeply expressive. The intimacy of the small format is to be savored like a fine wine and explored with a full sensory palette. Come close and breathe deeply — Øyvind Hjelmen's images unfold and expand. Each glimpse reveals another layer of charm and grace.

Elsewhere is a magical passage that enriches all who make the journey with an open heart.

— *Tracy Xavia Karner*

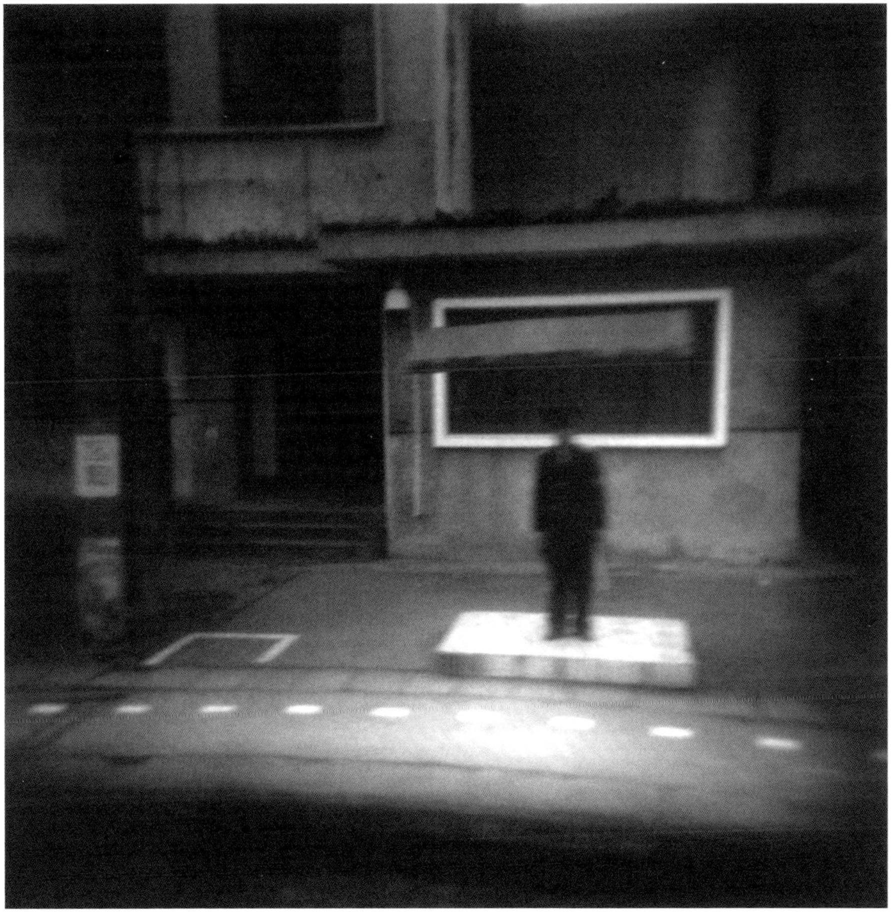

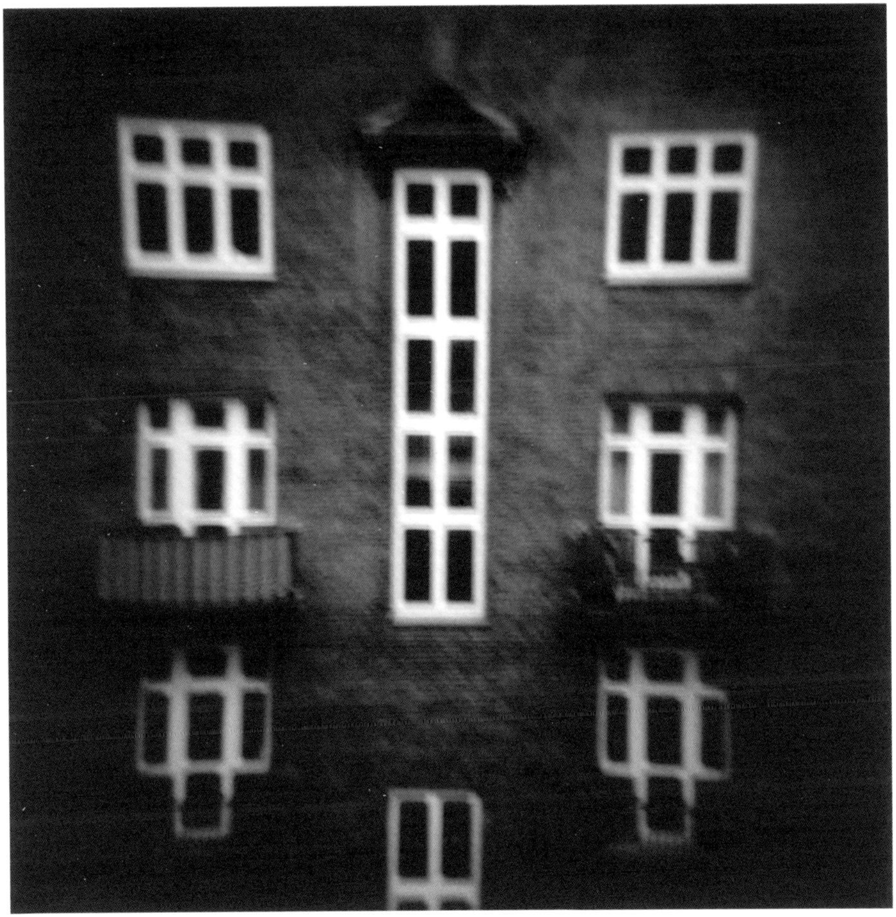

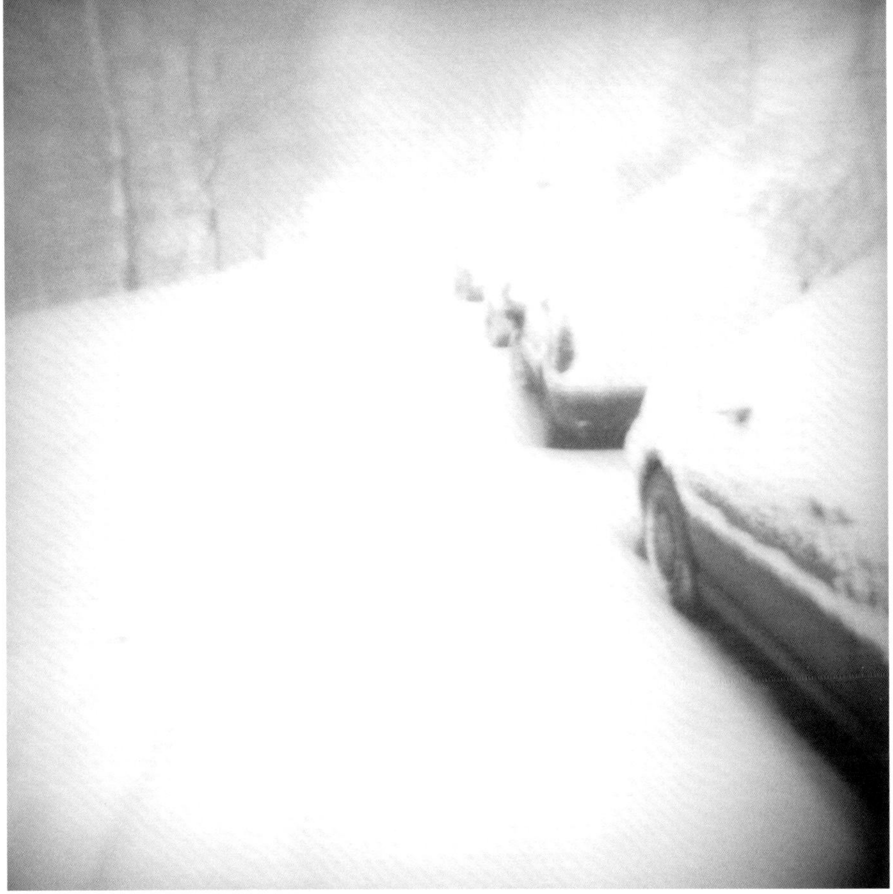

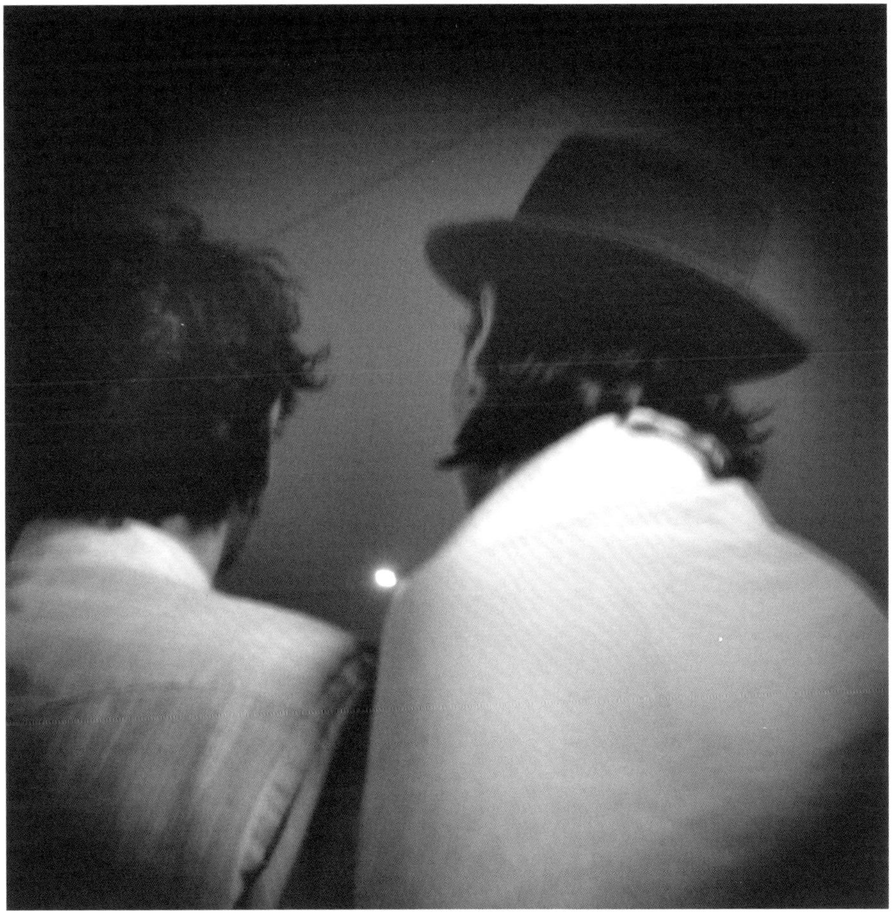

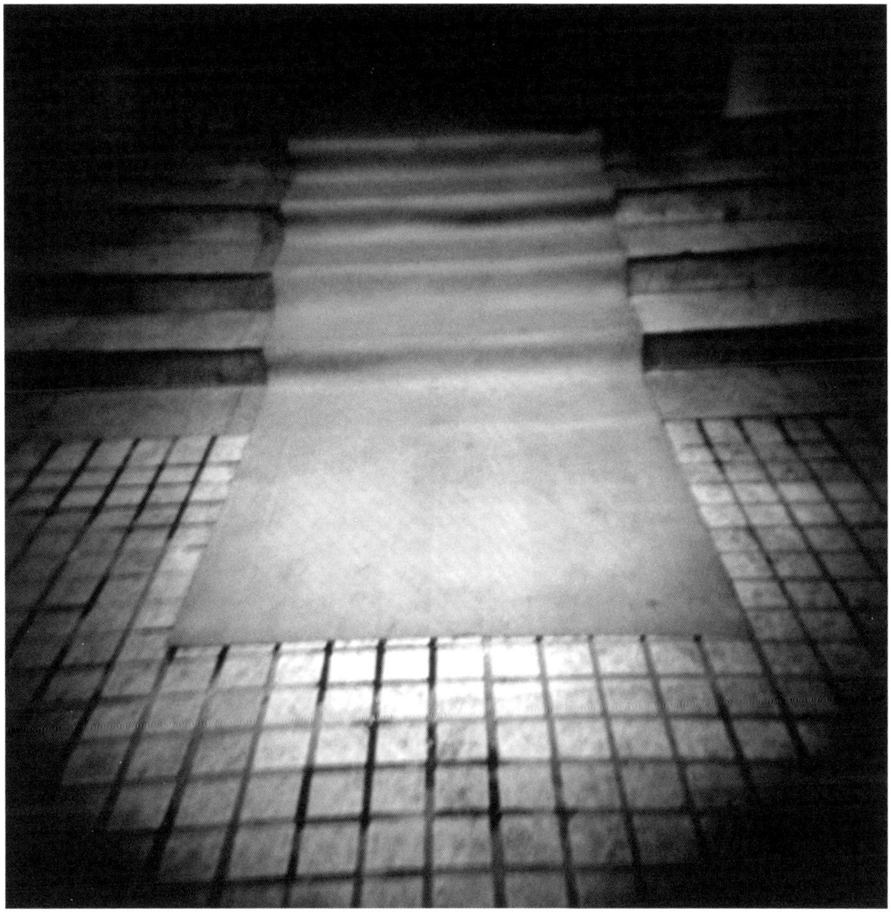

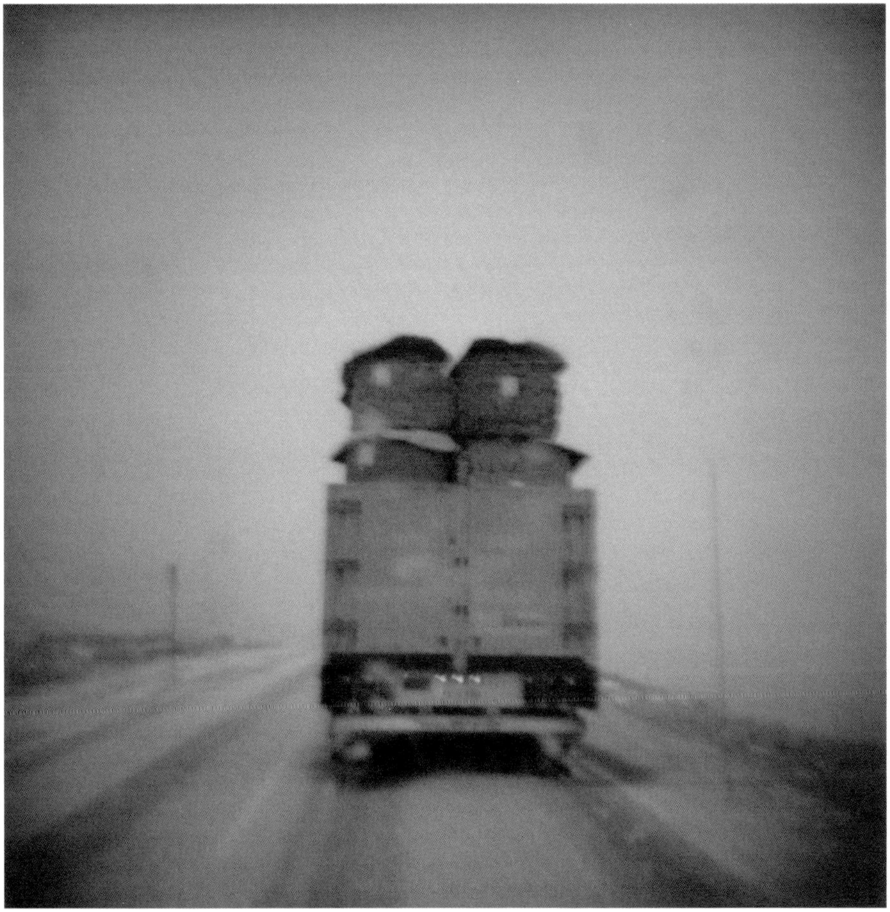

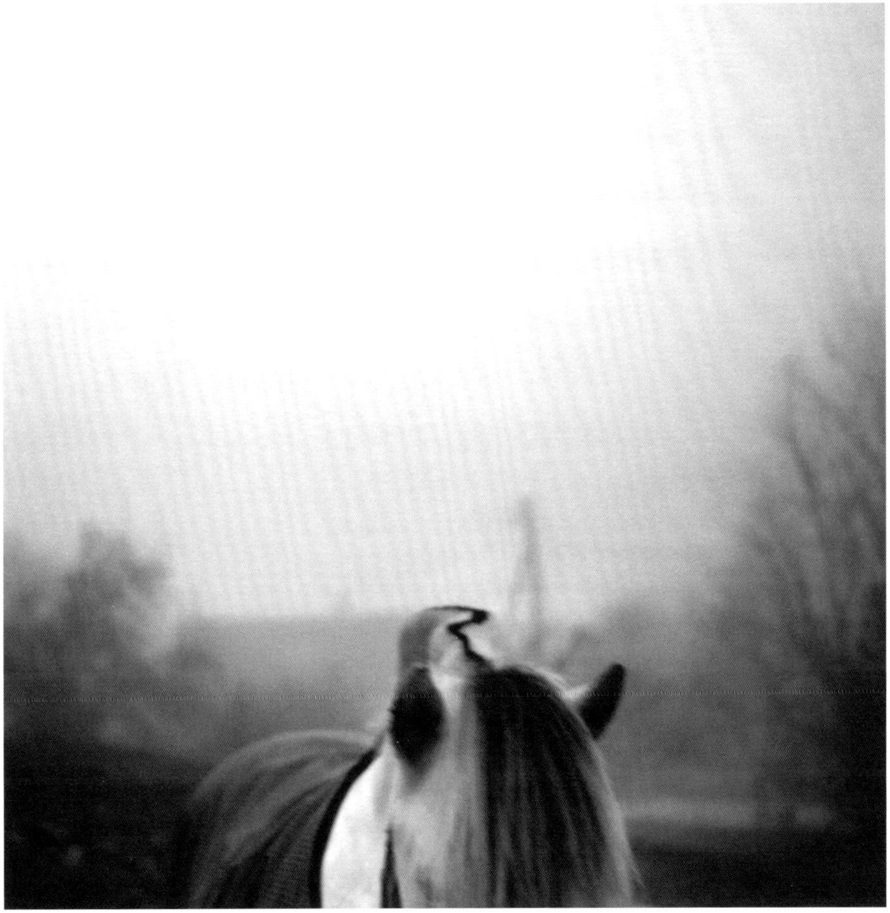

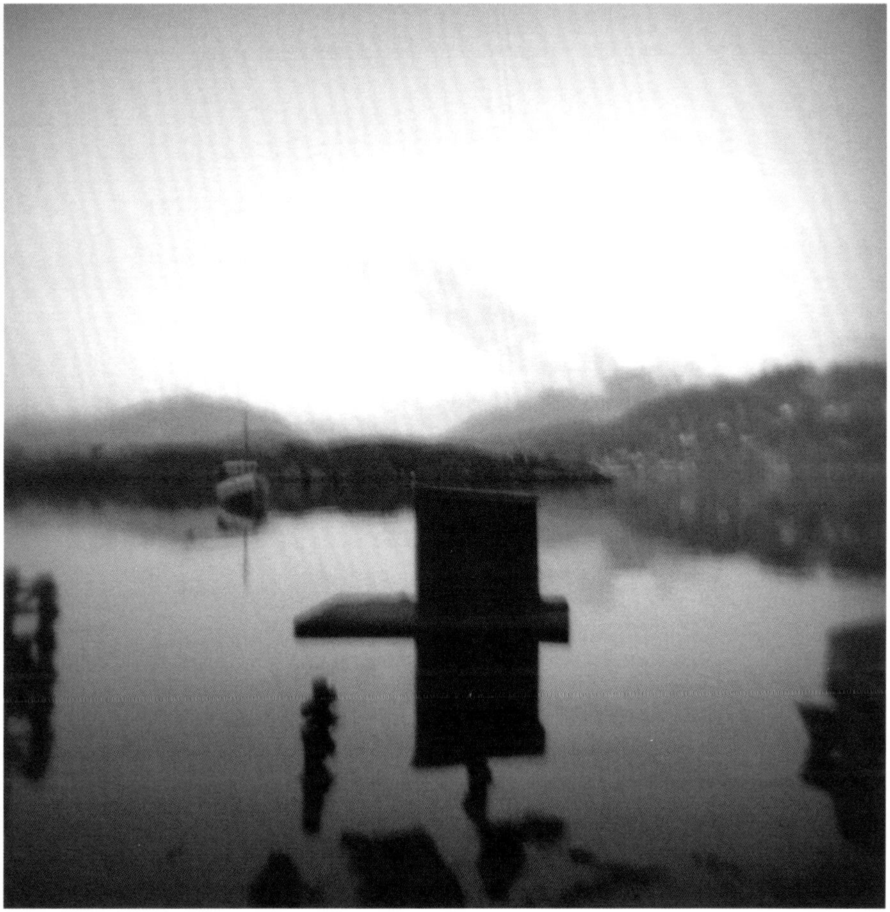

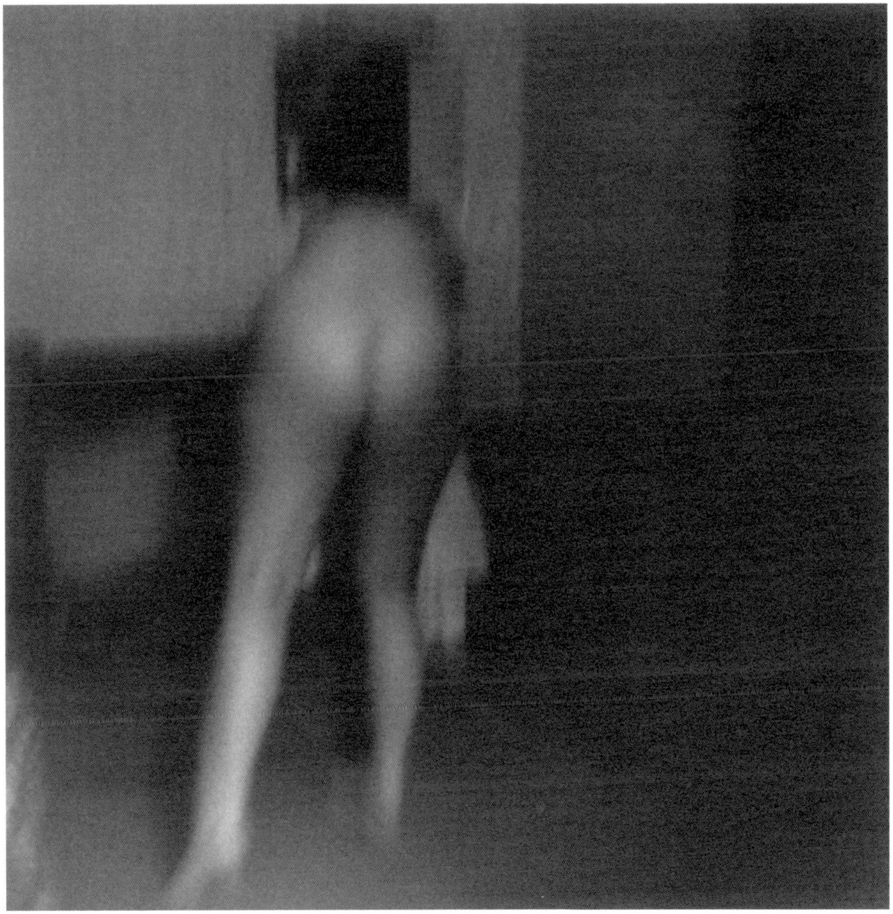

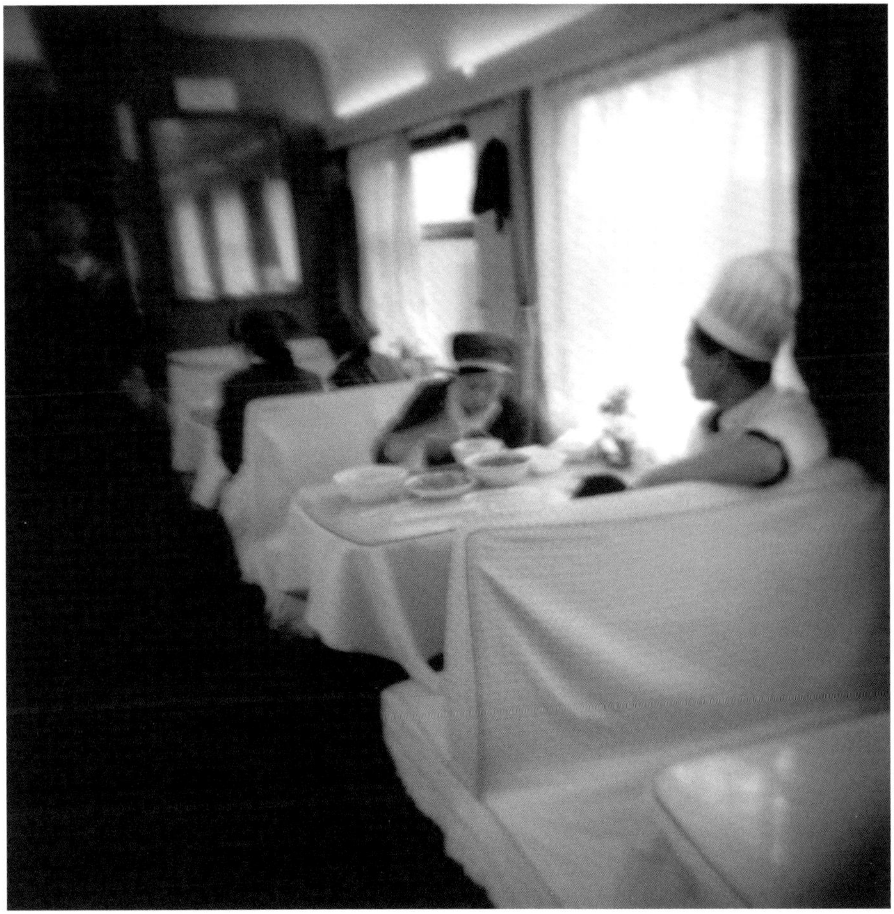

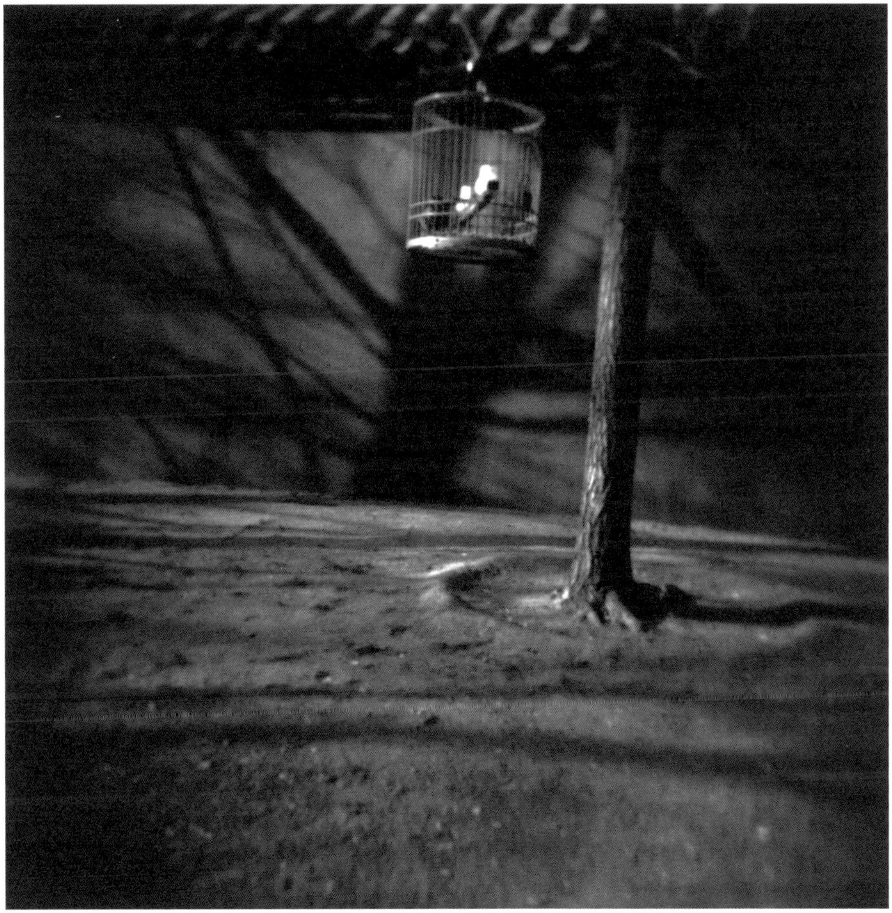

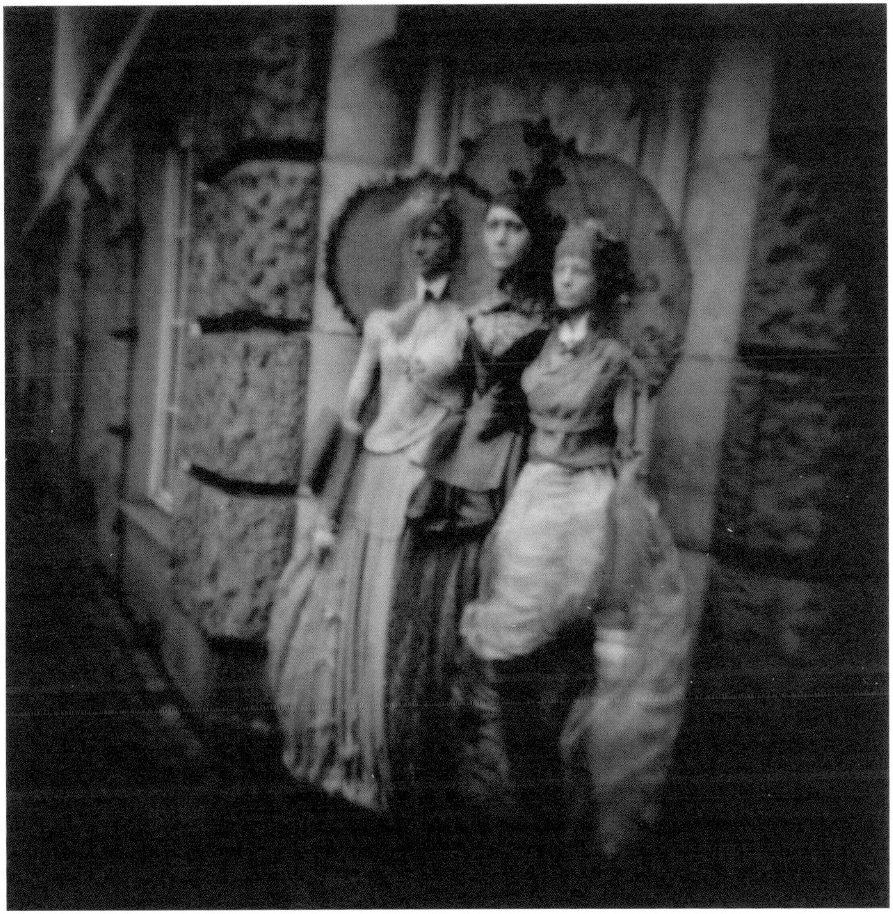

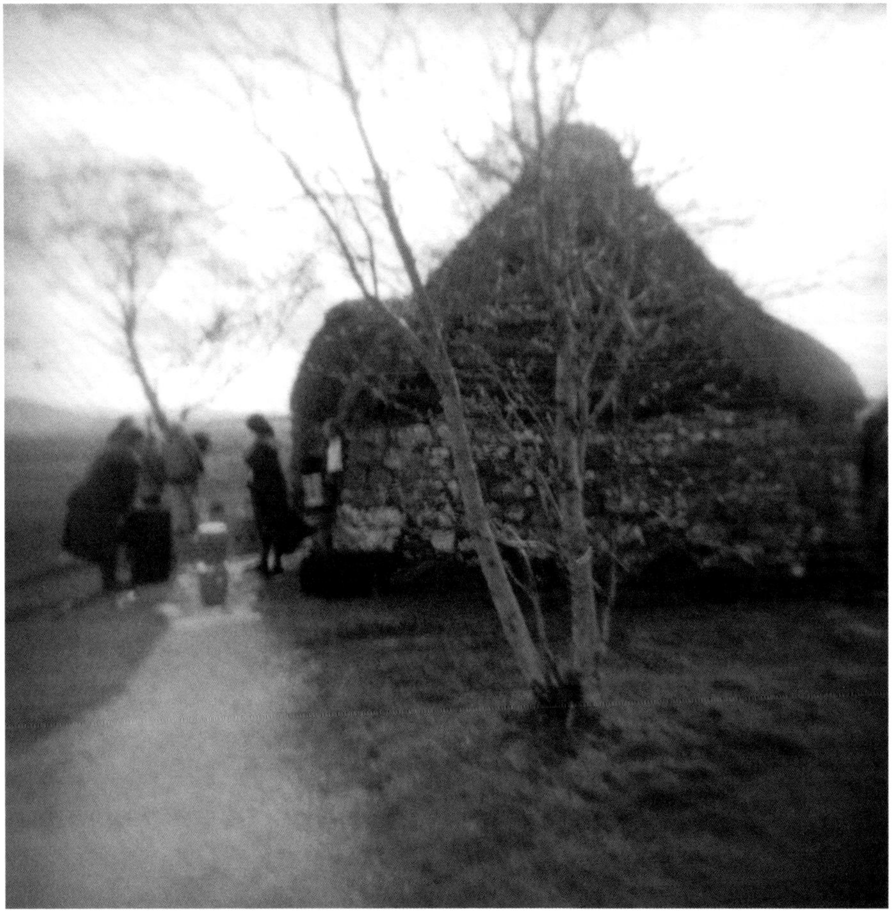

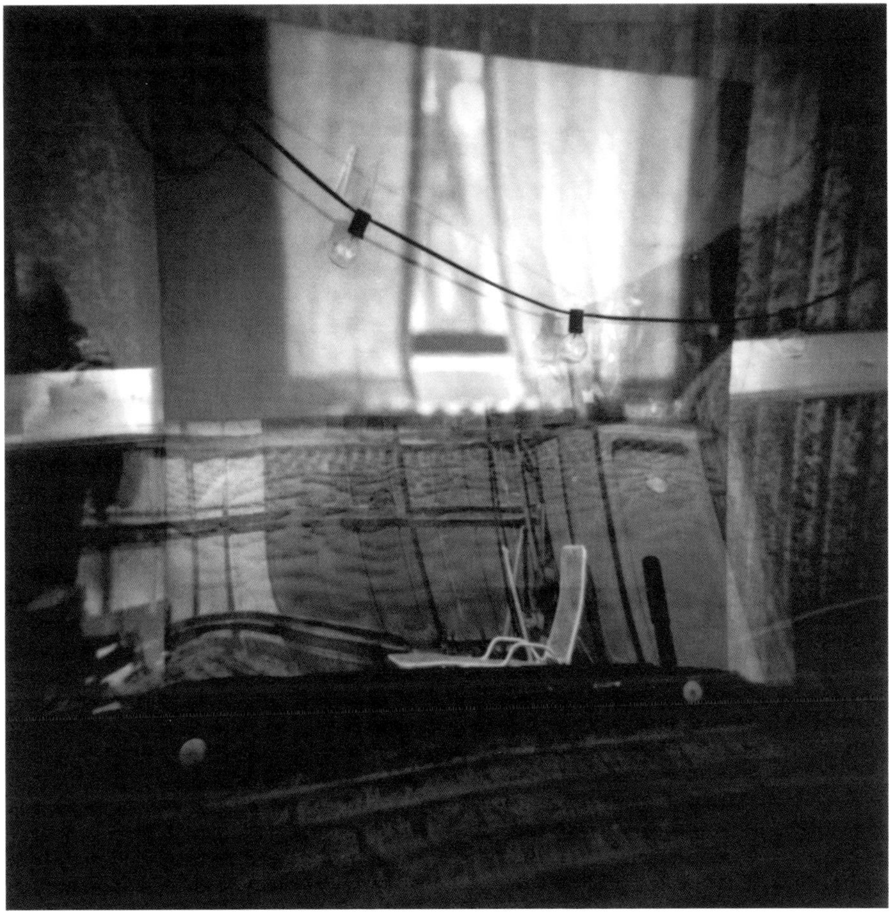

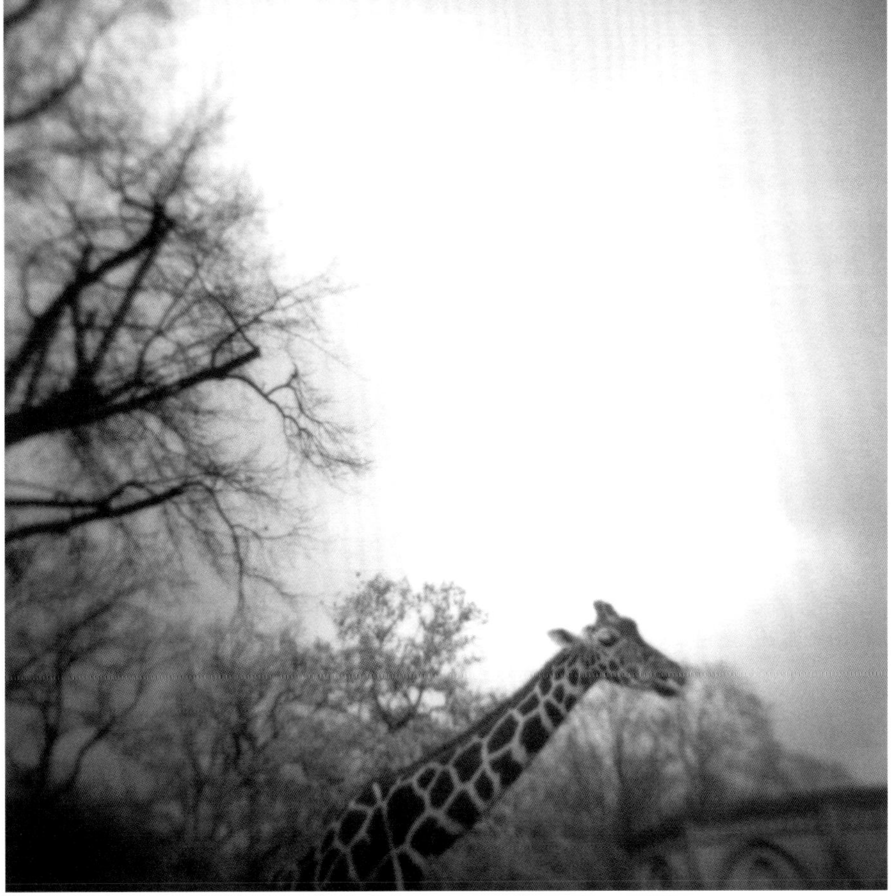

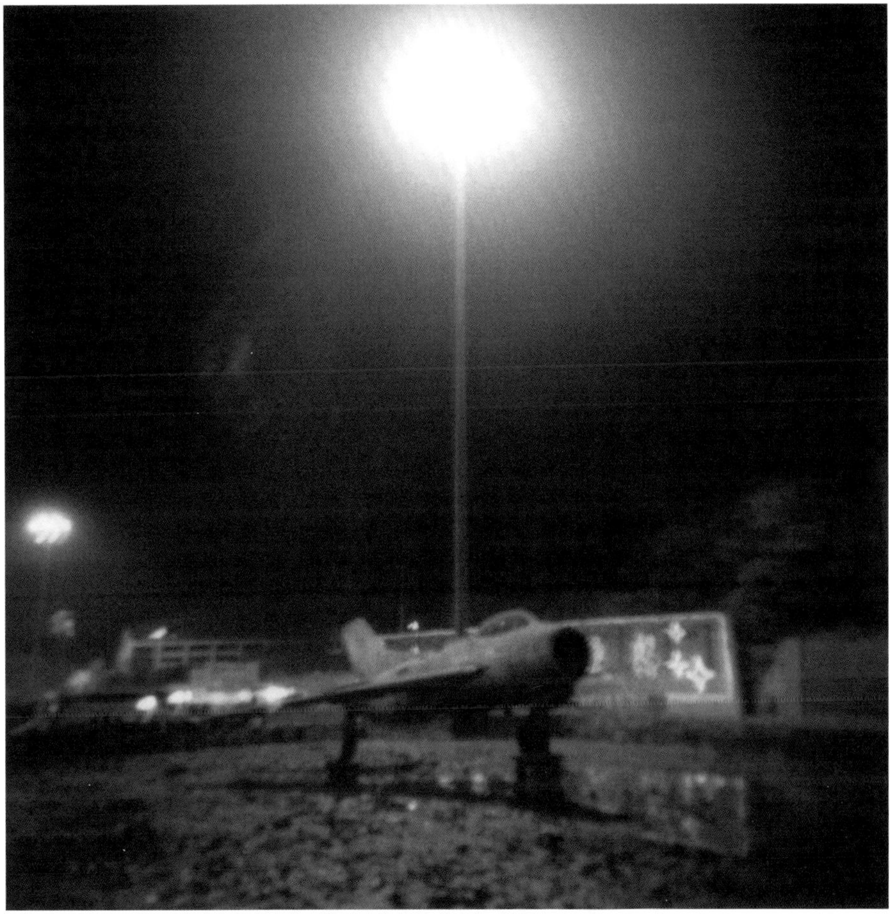

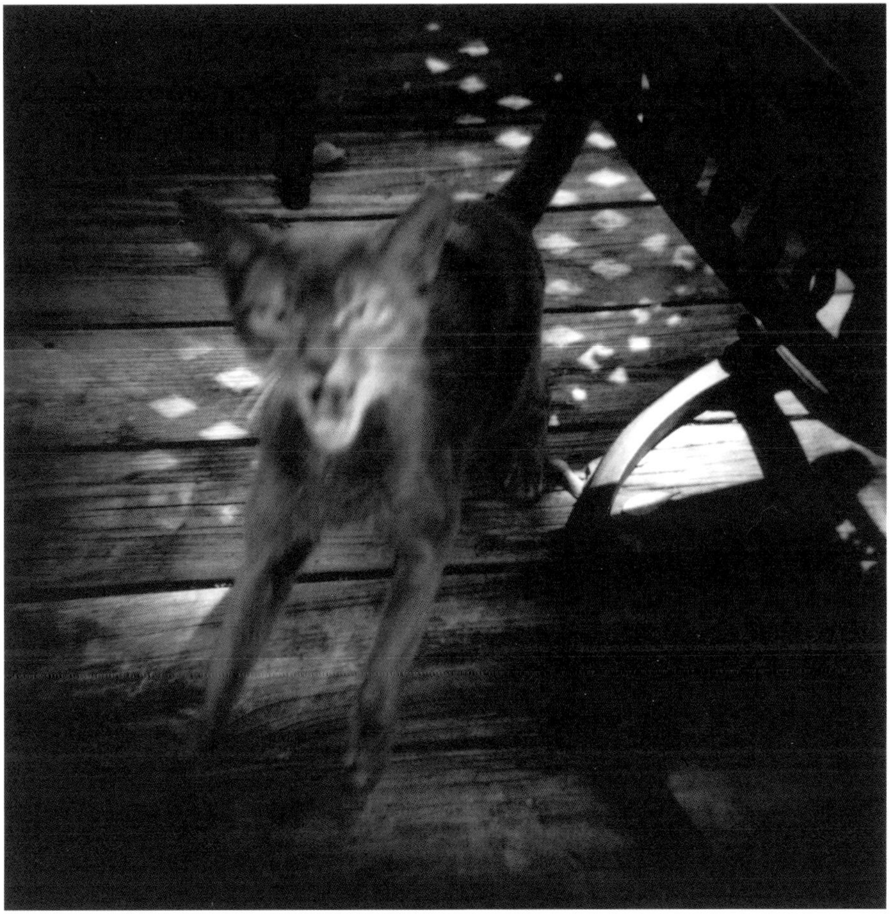

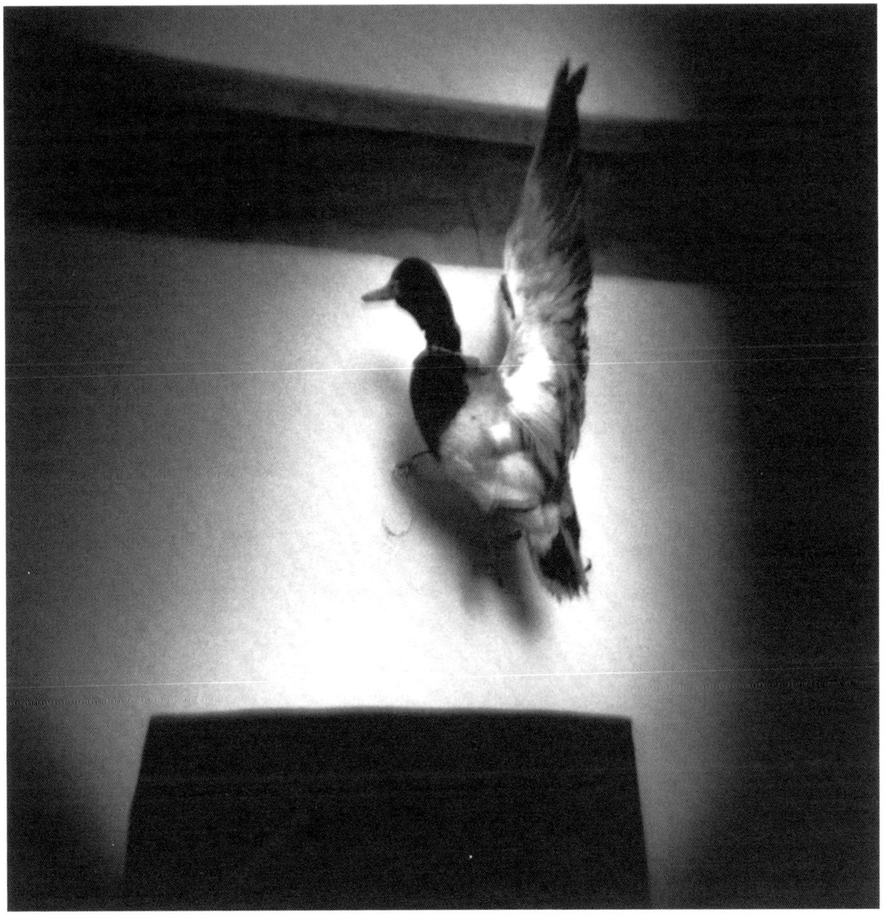

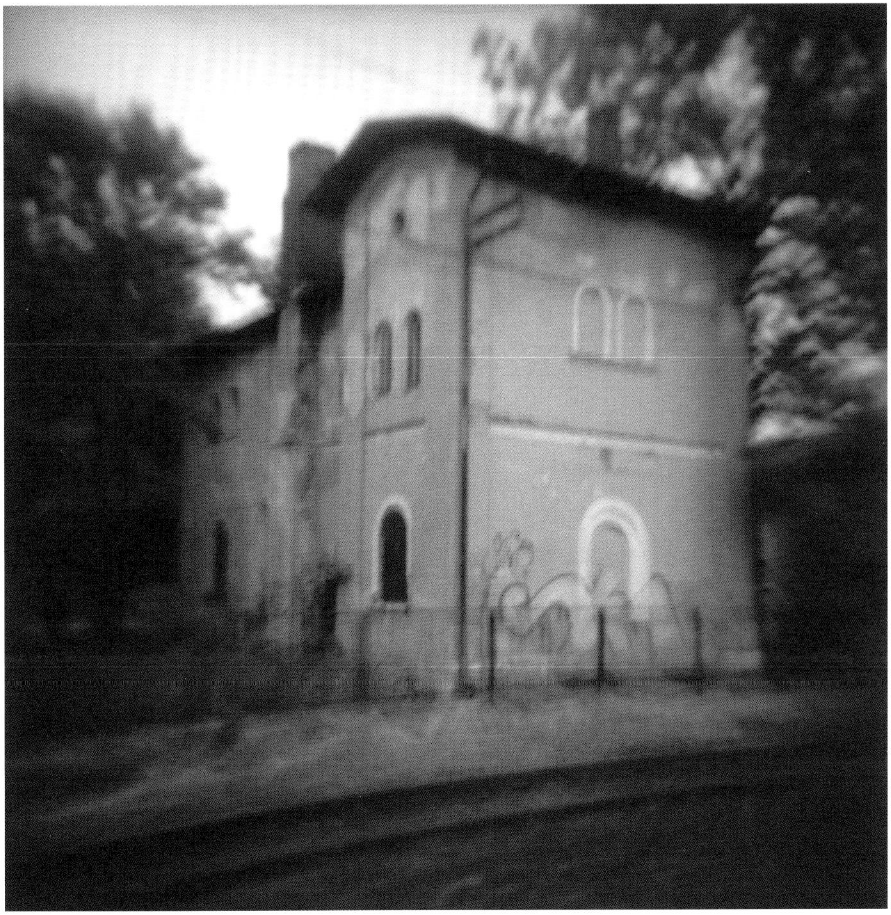

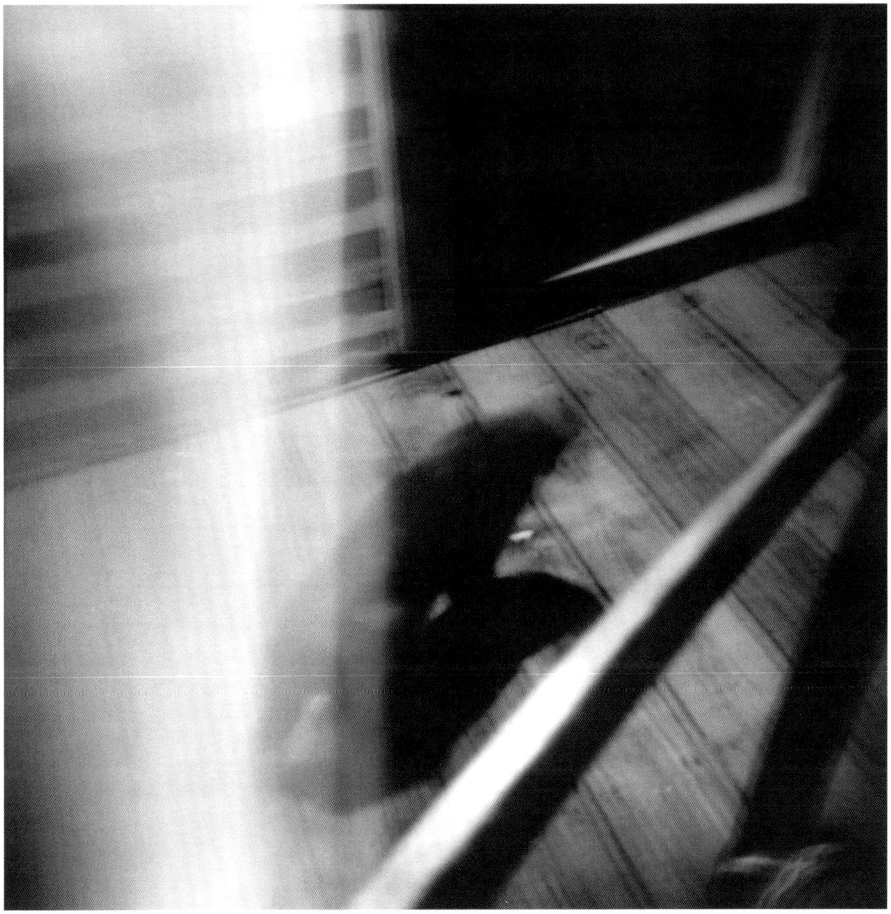

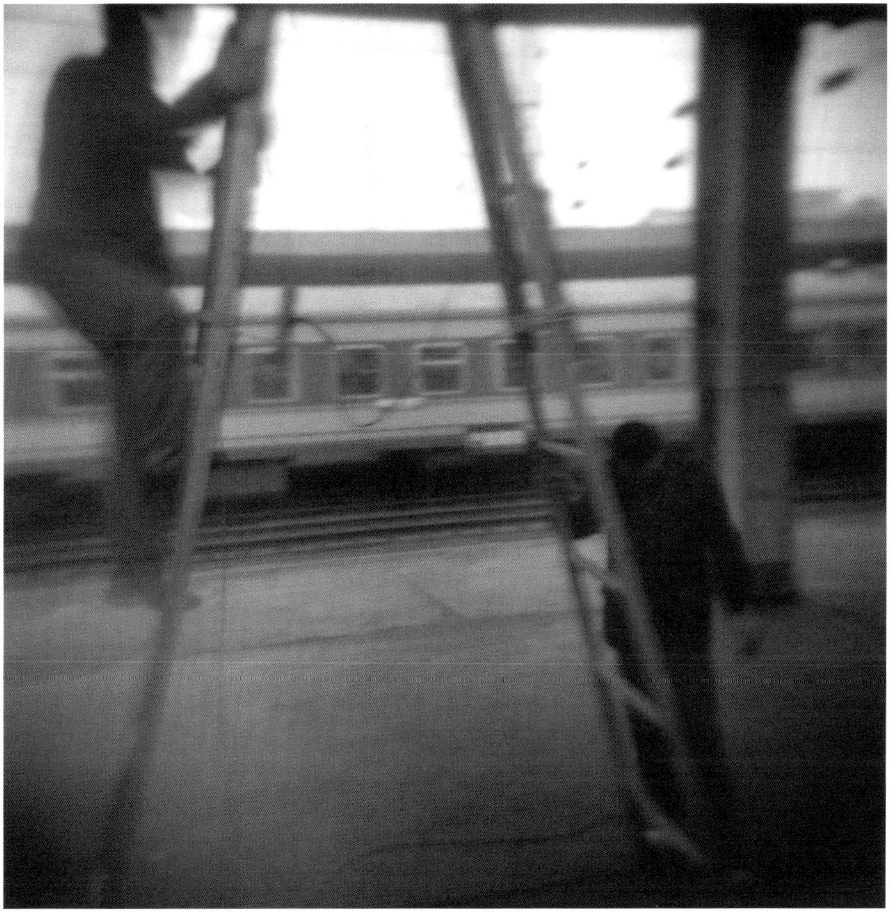

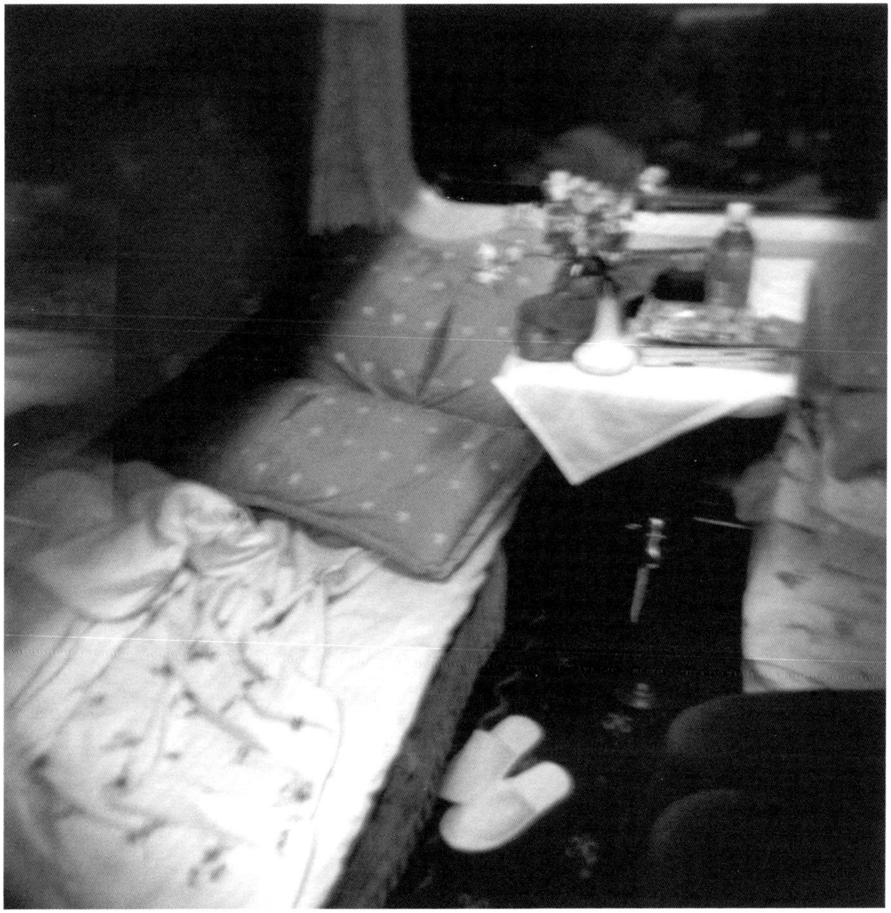

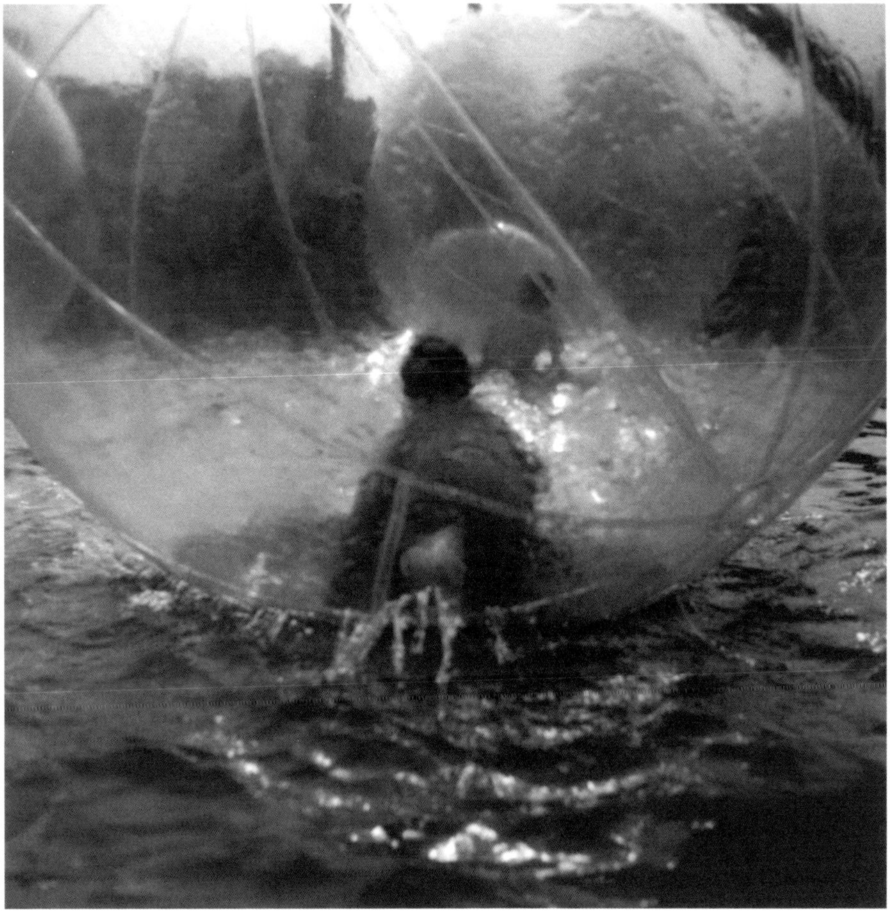

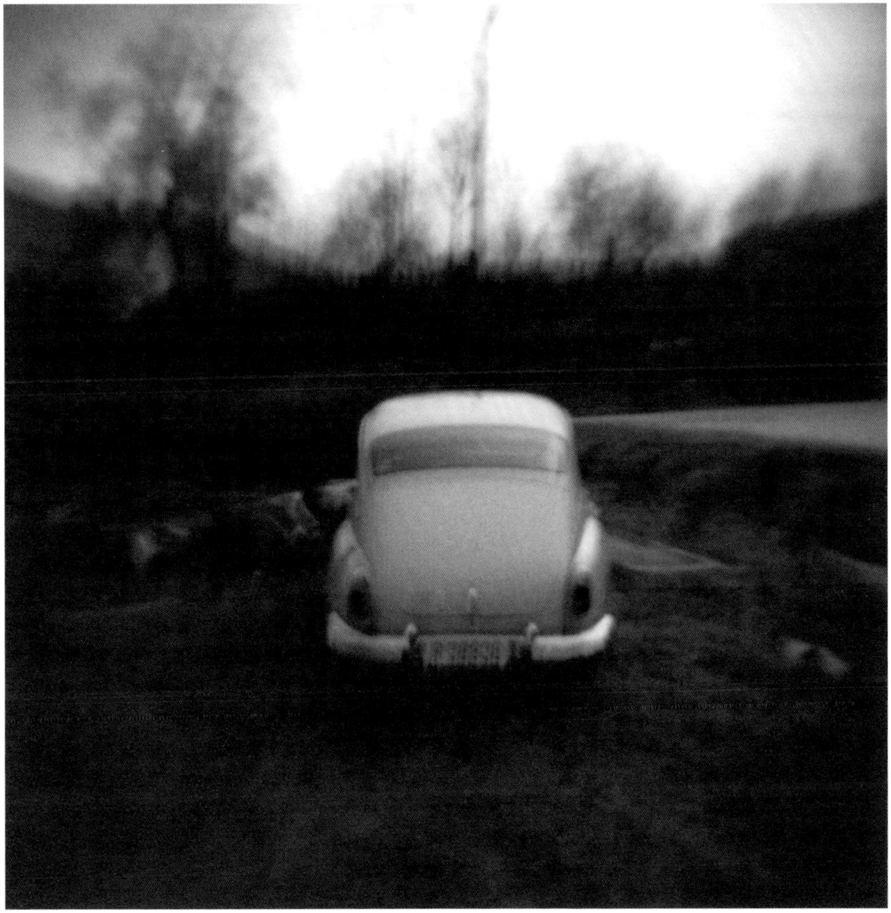

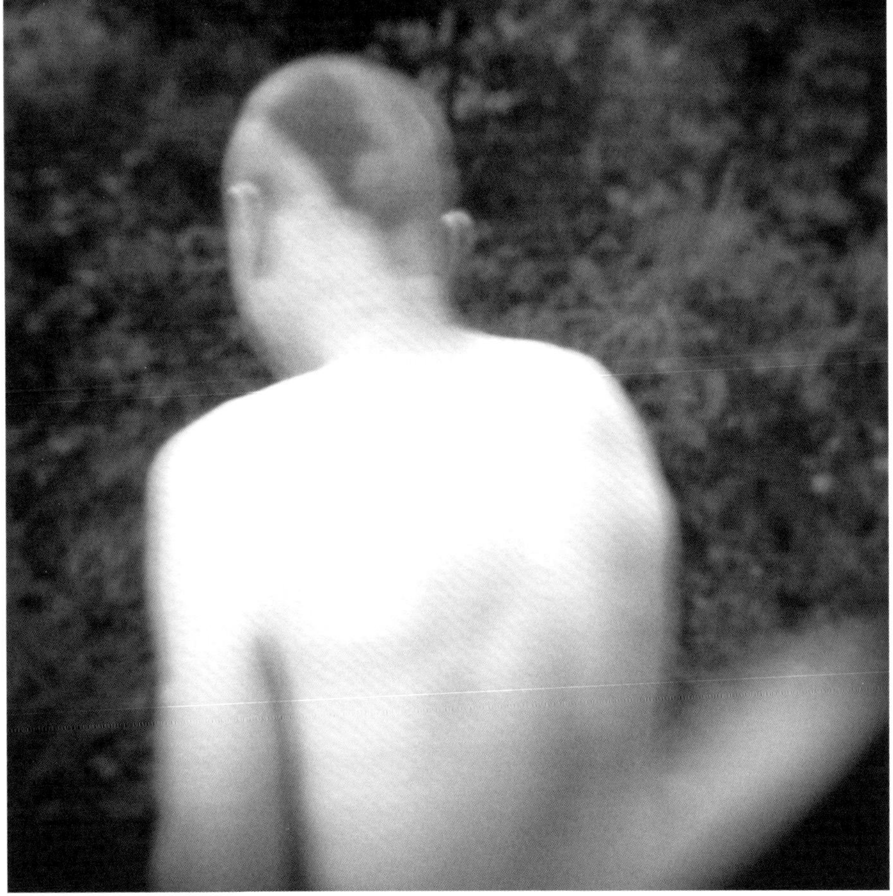

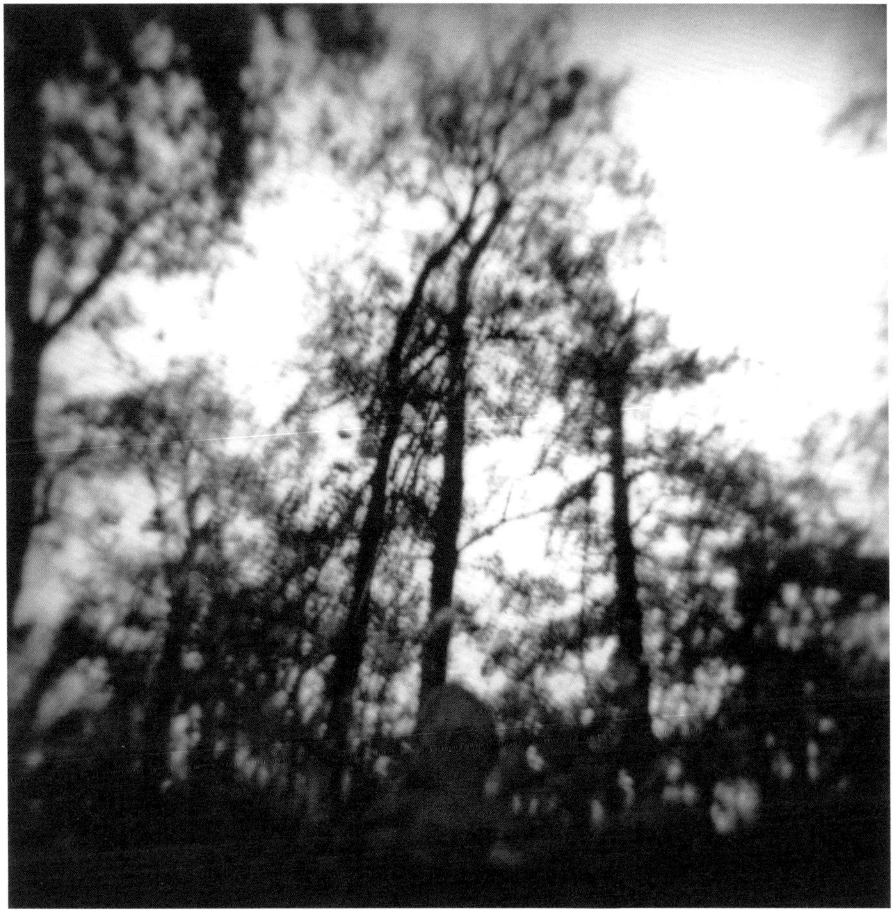

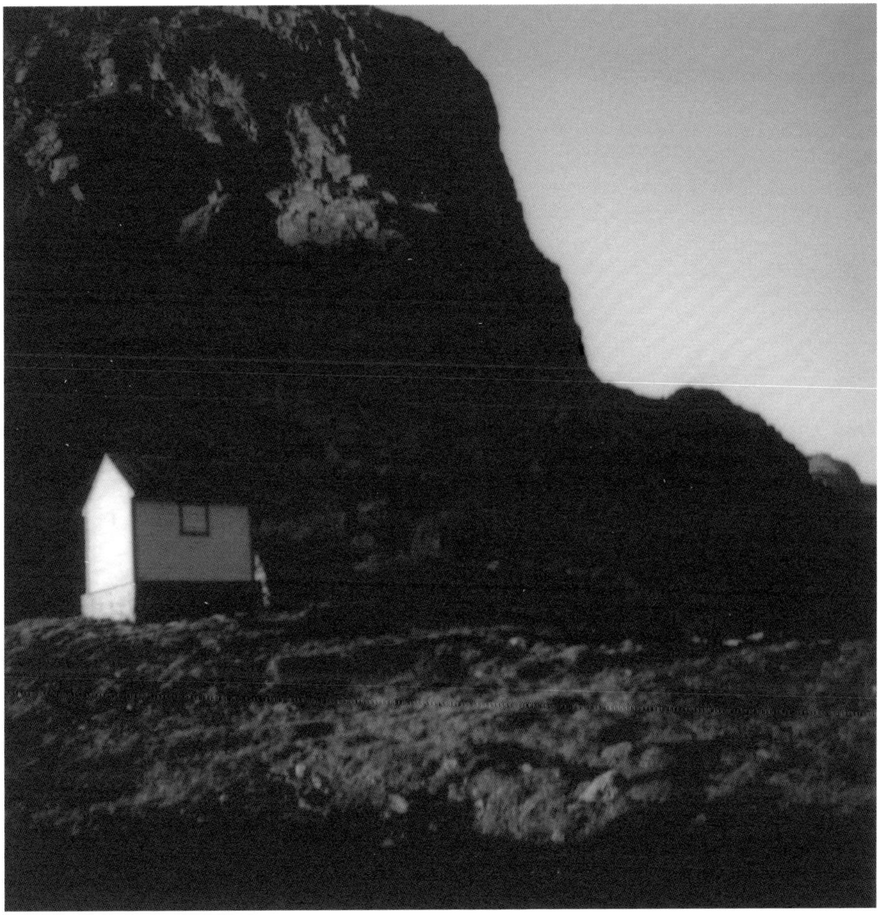

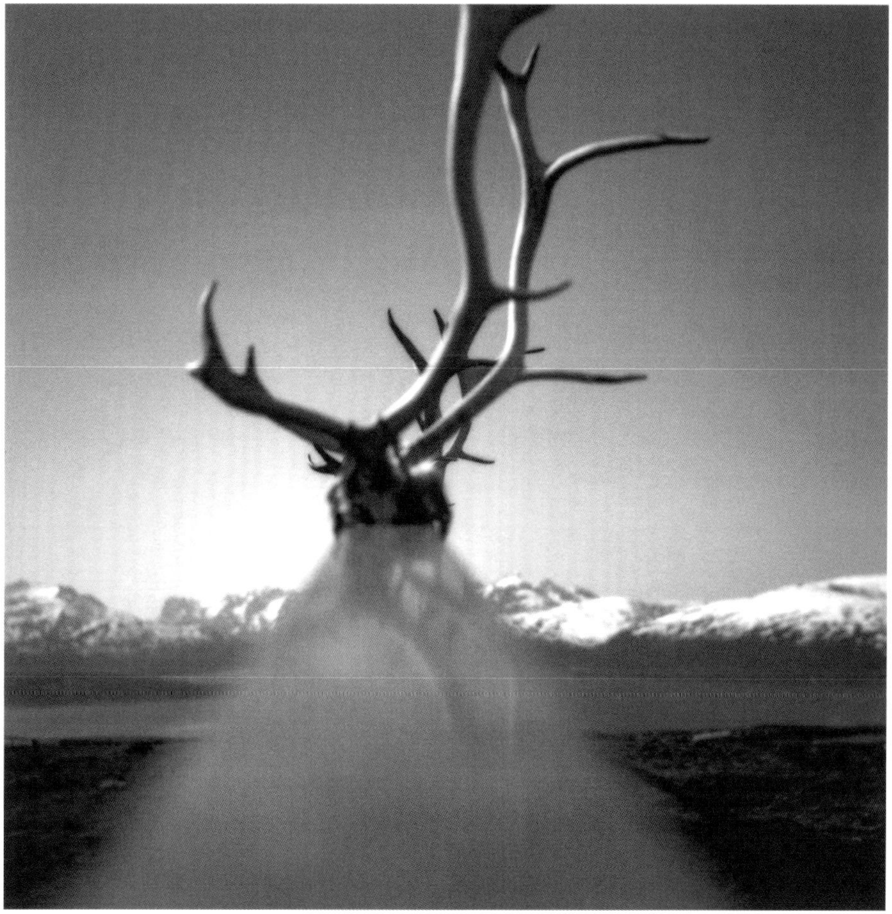

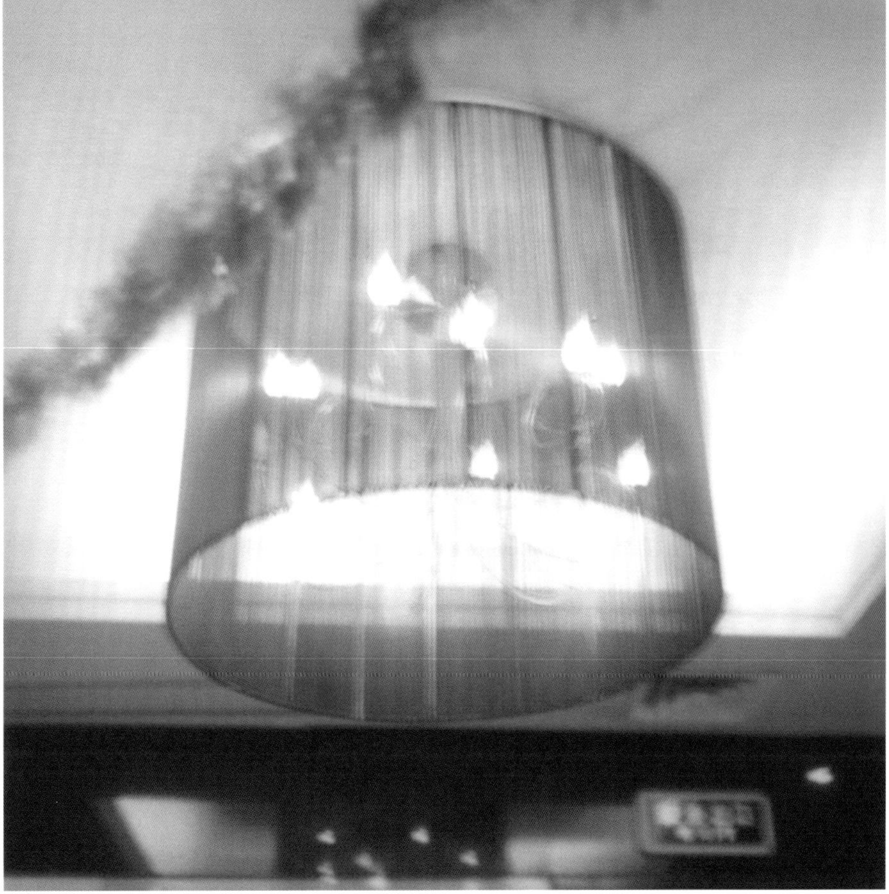

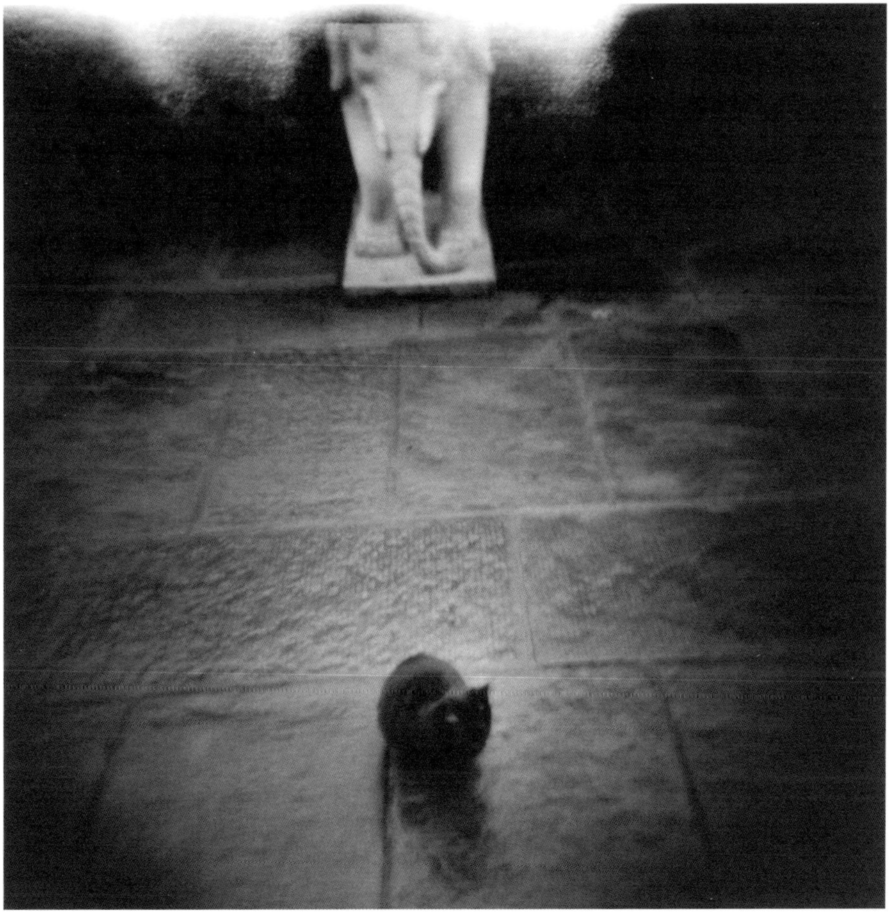

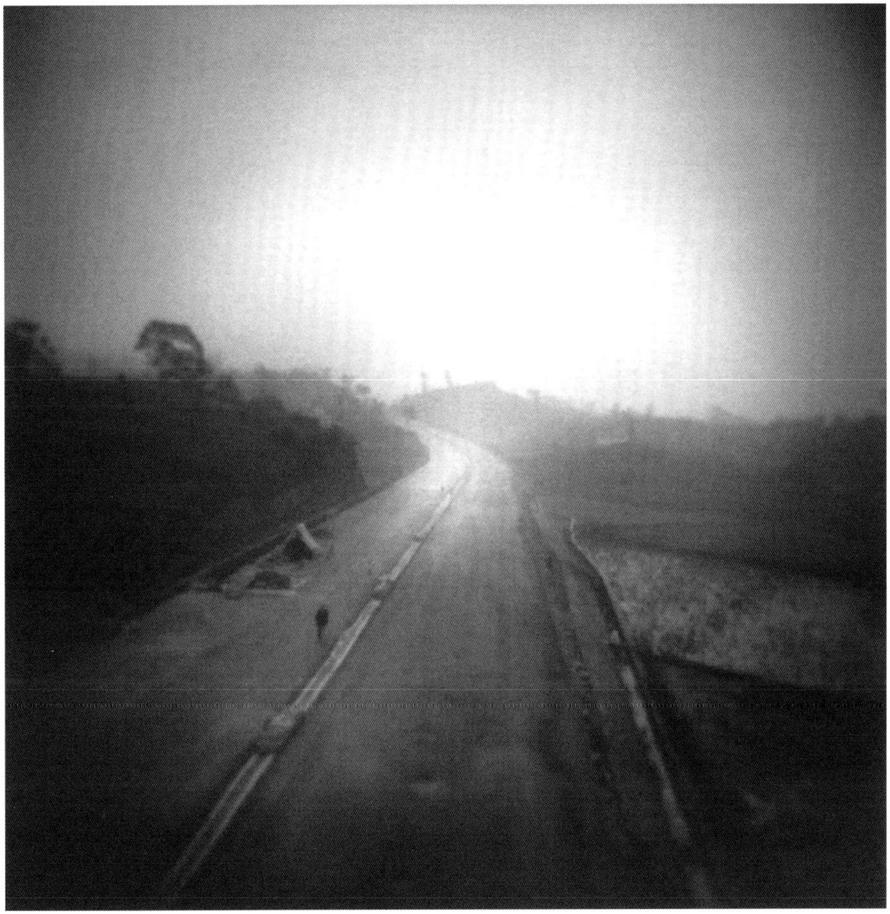

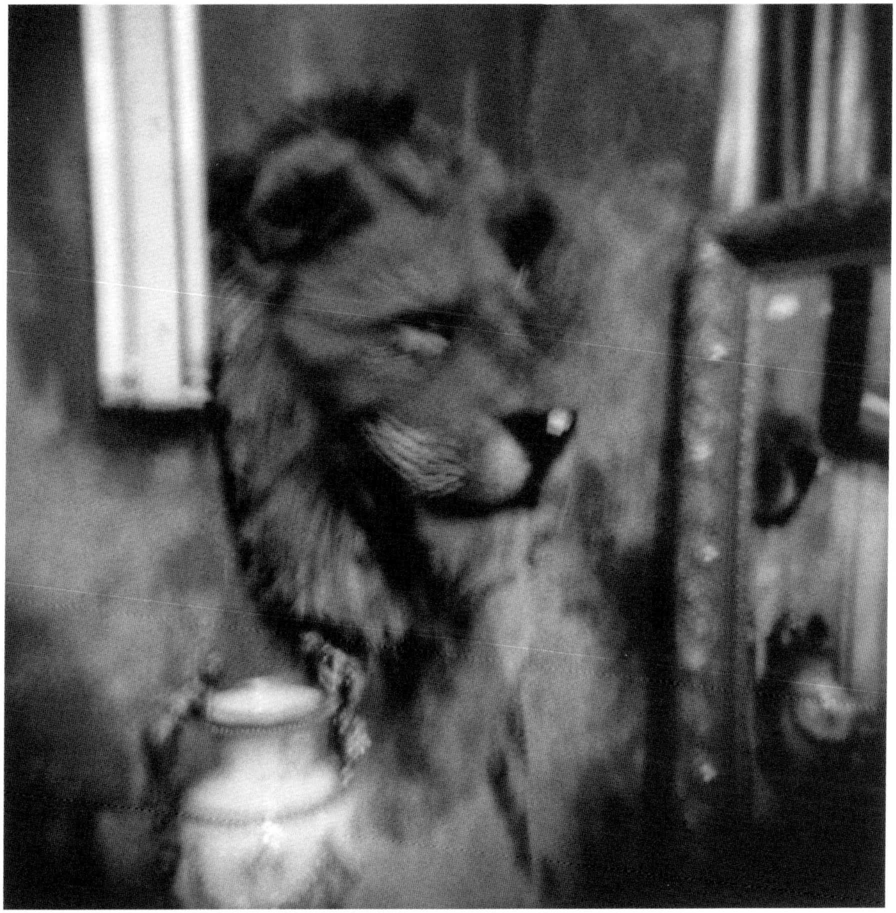

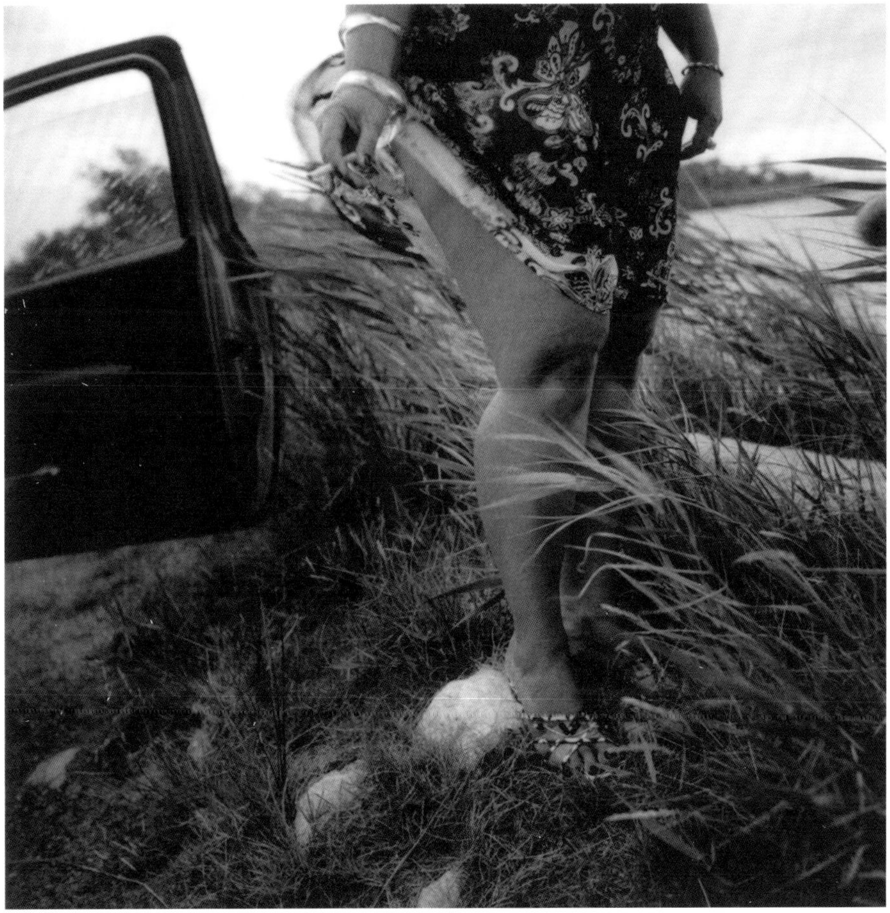

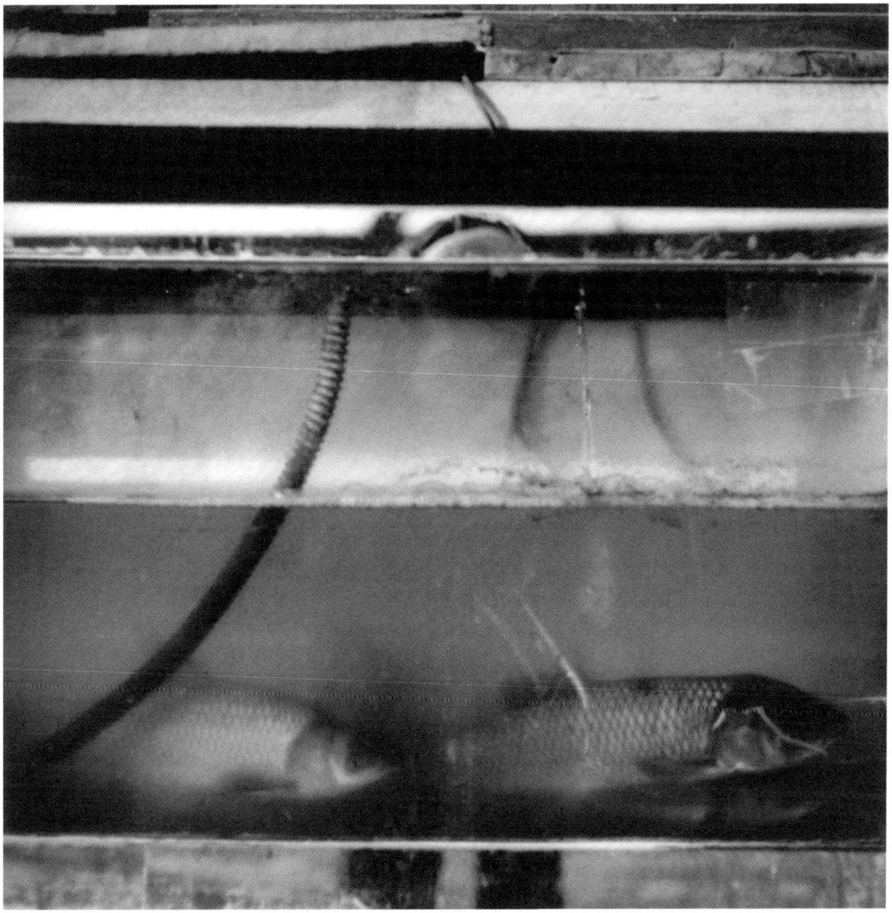

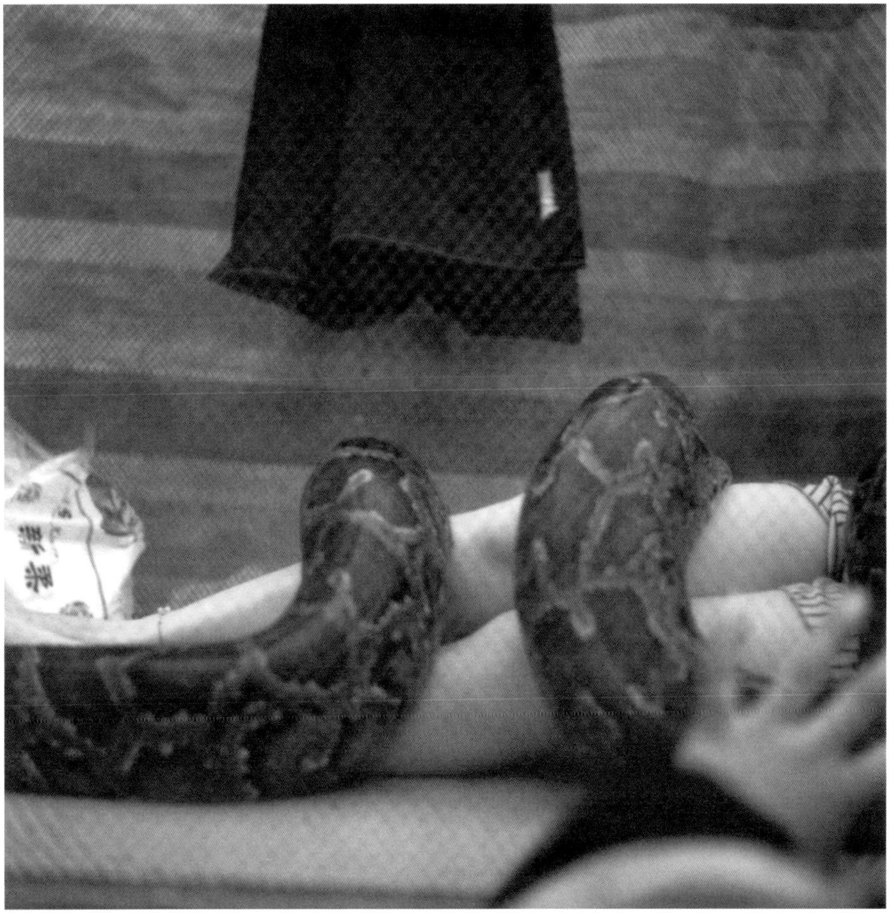

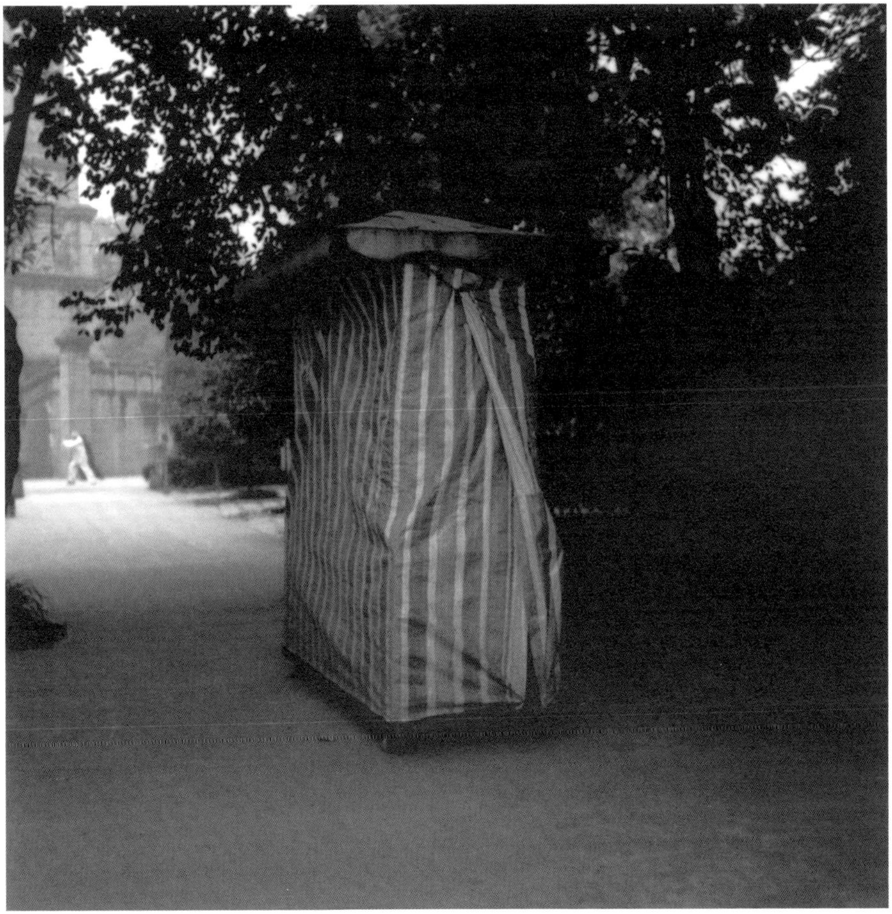

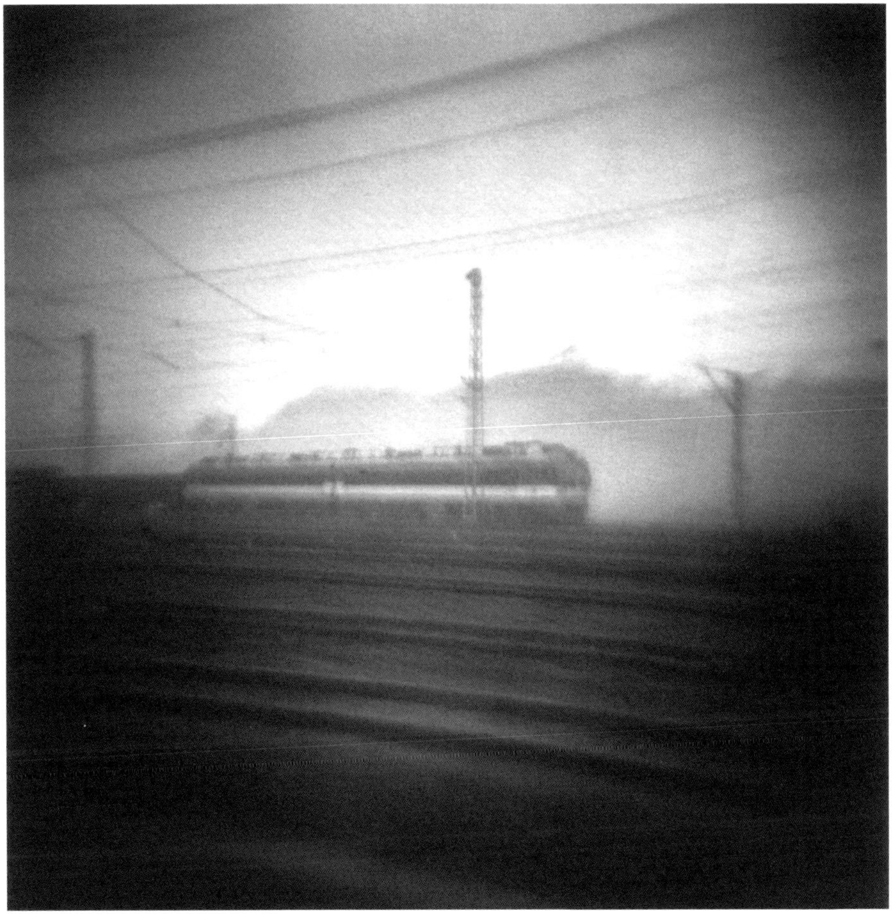

ARTIST BIOGRAPHY

Øyvind Hjelmen lives and works on the island of Stord, off the west coast of Norway. Apart from having attended various photographic workshops, he is autodidactic as an artist. He holds a BA in modern art and aesthetics from the University of Bergen.

Øyvind Hjelmen has been working with photography as his artistic expression for more than 15 years, and his works have been exhibited in the USA, Germany, Russia, United Kingdom, Poland, Lithuania, Greece, Italy, Japan, France and Norway. Among the collections that hold his works are The Museum of Fine Art in Houston, Texas, USA, and Centro Internazionale di Fotografia Scavi Scaligeri, Verona, Italy.

His black and white photographs are all film-based gelatin silver prints, handmade by the artist. His color works are film-based giclée fine art prints.

www.oyvindhjelmen.com

TRACY XAVIA KARNER

Tracy Xavia Karner, PhD, is an author, curator, visual artist and photo-obsessed sociologist with a background in Painting, Textile Arts, and Photography as well as graduate degrees in Sociology. She has published numerous articles and essays on art, photography and culture in popular and academic venues and is currently the Chair of the Sociology Department at the University of Houston in Houston, Texas, USA.

My sincere thanks to:

Catherine Cameron

Tracy Xavia Karner, my dear friends Millie and Jim Casper,
Alexa Becker, Aase Gundersen, and to Tone Elin Solholm for the design.

This book has been published thanks to generous support from Aker Solutions.

Photographs: Øyvind Hjelmen

Foreword: Tracy Xavia Karner

Design: Tone Elin Solholm / Kairos Works

Production: Kehrer Design Heidelberg

Paper: BVS Matt

ISBN: 978-3-86828-198-9

Kehrer Verlag

Heidelberg Berlin